Una Locke

Star-Flowers

Una Locke

Star-Flowers

ISBN/EAN: 9783337038151

Printed in Europe, USA, Canada, Australia, Japan

Cover: Foto ©Lupo / pixelio.de

More available books at **www.hansebooks.com**

STAR-FLOWERS

URANIA LOCKE BAILEY

Though the warm breath of summer lingered still
 In the lone paths where late her footsteps passed,
The pallid star-flowers on the purple hill
 Sighed dreamily, "We are the last! the last!"
                                        SARAH HELEN WHITMAN.

NEW YORK
G. P. PUTNAM'S SONS
27 & 29 WEST 23D STREET
1882

CONTENTS.

	PAGE.
THE PRAISE-MEETING OF THE FLOWERS	1
CHRIST AND THE LITTLE ONES	6
THE OPEN DOOR	9
SAINT STEPHEN	11
STRANGE SURPRISES	13
BALLAD OF THE BOATS	16
THE MERRY MAY WEATHER	20
OUR MOTHER	22
LEFT BEHIND	24
OUR SISTER	26
THE MIDSUMMER CHILD	28
MEMORIES OF OUR FATHER	30
LU AND I	34
OUR POSSESSION	37
THE HOME VALLEY	39
EMILY	41
VALLEY OF THE HEART'S-EASE	43
THE POET'S FRIENDS	45
THE "CATTLE" TO THE "POET"	46
"INASMUCH"	47
THE HEART'S COMPLAINT	51
THE DREAM	54

CONTENTS.

	PAGE
DEAR EMILY	56
ROSSY	59
MARY	62
IN MEMORY OF L. J. R.	64
THE DEAR ONE DEAD	66
THE BROKEN SPELL	68
TO WHAT SHALL I LIKEN HER?	73
PRINCESS AND POET	75
1776	77
THE FALSE SECRET	79
THE BENEDICTION	81
OUT IN THE WILDERNESS	84
CHRIST IS IN THE UNIVERSE	87
THE BELOVED STRANGER	89
THE YOUNG MOTHER	91
WATCHING MOTHER	93
THE DEDICATION OF THE BABY	96
MOTHER'S SONG	100
FAIRY MAY	102
LITTLE JULIA	105
LITTLE WILLIE	107
THE BEREAVED MOTHER	108
THE SLAVE MOTHER	111
THE SAVIOUR TO THE SORROWFUL SOUL	113
THE UNSEEN KINGDOM	115
AMONG THE RUSHES	118
THE UNSEEN GUARD	122
AMONG THE LIONS	125
THE VISIT OF THE ANGELS	130

CONTENTS.

	PAGE.
THE BLESSED MASTER	134
ON THE WATER	135
A SONG FOR SORROWFUL WOMEN	138
THE PRAYER-MEETING FOR PETER	140
I WISHED MYSELF AMONG THEM	145
THE LORD'S DAY	147
OUT OF THE NIGHT	149
TWENTY-FOUR AND SIXTY	151

STAR-FLOWERS.

THE PRAISE–MEETING OF THE FLOWERS.

THE flowers of many climates,
   That bloom all seasons through,
Met in a stately garden
   Bright with the morning dew.

For praise and loving worship
   The Lord they came to meet;
Her box of precious perfume
   The Rose broke at His feet.

The Passion-flower His symbols
   Wore fondly on her breast;
She spoke of self-denial
   As what might please Him best.

The Morning-glories, fragile,
    Like infants soon to go,
Had dainty toy-like trumpets,
    And praised the Master so.

"His word is like to honey,"
    The Clover testified;
"And all who trust His promise
    Shall in His love abide."

The Lilies said: "Oh, trust Him!
    We neither toil nor spin,
And yet His house of beauty
    See how we enter in!"

The Kingcup and her kindred
    Said: "Let us all be glad!
Of His redundant sunshine
    Behold how we are clad!"

"And let us follow Jesus,"
    The Star of Bethlehem said;
And all the band of star-flowers
    Bent down with reverent head.

The giant Sunflower answered,
    And little Daisies bright,
And all the cousin Asters :
    "We follow toward the Light !"

"We praise Him for the mountains !"
    The Alpine Roses cried ;
"We bless Him for the valleys,"
    The Violets replied.

"We praise Him," said the Air-plants,
    "For breath we never lack";
"And for the rocks we praise Him,"
    The Lichens answered back.

"We praise God for the waters,"
    The salt Sea-mosses sighed ;
And all His baptized Lilies
    "Amen ! Amen !" replied.

"And for the cool green woodlands
    We praise and thanks return,"
Said Kalmias and Azaleas
    And graceful feathery Fern.

"And for the wealth of gardens
    And all the gardener thinks,"
Said Roses and Camellias
    And all the sweet-breathed Pinks.

"Hosanna in the highest!"
    The baby Bluets sang;
And little trembling Harebells
    With softest music rang.

"The winter hath been bitter,
    But sunshine follows storm;
Thanks for His loving-kindness,
    The earth's great heart is warm."

So said the pilgrim's Mayflower
    That cometh after snow,
The humblest and the sweetest
    Of all the flowers that blow.

"Thank God for every weather,
    The sunshine and the wet,"
Spoke out the cheery Pansies
    And darling Mignonette.

And then the sun descended,
    The heavens were all aglow;
The little Morning-glories
    Had faded hours ago.

And now the bright Day-lilies
    Their love-watch ceased to keep;
"He giveth," said the Poppies,
    "To His beloved, sleep."

The gray of evening deepened,
    A soft wind stirred the corn;
When sudden in the garden
    Another flower was born!

It was the Evening Primrose;
    Her sisters followed fast;
With perfumed lips they whispered:
    "Thank God for night at last!"

CHRIST AND THE LITTLE ONES.

"THE Master has come over Jordan,"
   Said Hannah, the mother, one day;
"He is healing the people who throng Him
   With a touch of His finger, they say.
And so I shall carry the children,
   Little Rachel, and Samuel, and John;
I shall carry the baby Esther,
   For the Lord to look upon."

The father looked at her kindly,
   But he shook his head and smiled;
"Ah! who but a doting mother
   Would think of a thing so wild?
If the children were tortured by demons,
   Or dying of fever, 't were well;
Or had they the taint of the leper,
   Like many in Israel."

"Nay, do not hinder me, Nathan!
   I feel such a burden of care;

If I carry it to the Master
    Perhaps I shall leave it there.
If He lay His hand on the children
    My heart will be lighter, I know,
For a blessing forever and ever
    Will follow them as they go."

So over the hills of Judah,
    Along by the vine-rows green,
With Esther asleep on her bosom,
    And Rachel her brothers between;
'Mong the people who hung on His teaching,
    Or waited His touch or His word;
Through the row of proud Pharisees listening,
    She pressed to the feet of the Lord.

"Now why shouldst thou hinder the Master,"
    Said Peter, "with children like these?
Seest not how from morning to evening
    He teacheth, and healeth disease?"
Then Christ said: "Forbid not the children;
    Permit them to come unto ME";
And He took in His arms little Esther,
    And Rachel He set on His knee.

>   And the heavy heart of the mother
>   Was lifted all earth-care above,
>   As He laid His hands on the brothers
>   And blessed them with tenderest love ;—
>   As He said of the babes in His bosom :
>   " Of such is the Kingdom of Heaven " ;
>   And strength for all duty and trial
>   That hour to her spirit was given.

Extract from a letter from Rev. Wm. Goodell, D.D., of Constantinople, Turkey, to Rev. Dr. Prime, of New York :

"I come to ask a special favor of you, viz.: that you will see that sweet singer in Israel, and composer, Mr.——, and ask him to make a tune for that beautiful hymn beginning with, 'The Master has come over Jordan.' The tune should be a very simple one, and suited to the popular ear, that all Christian mothers in the world may learn to sing it by hearing it once. We shall pray that Brother—— may be where John was 'on the Lord's day' (not in exile, but in the spirit), and may be assisted to make a tune which shall be sung in every land by every tongue, not only till the beginning of the Millennium, but straight through till the very end of it, and even far beyond."

THE OPEN DOOR.

THE mistakes of my life are many,
   The sins of my heart are more,
And I scarce can see for weeping,
   But I come to the open door.

I am lowest of those who love Him,
   I am weakest of those who pray;
But I come as He has bidden,
   And He will not say me nay.

My mistakes His love will cover,
   My sins He will wash away,
And the feet that shrink and falter
   Shall walk through the gate of day.

If I turn not from His whisper,
   If I let not go His hand,
I shall see Him in His beauty—
   The King in the far-off land.

The mistakes of my life are many,
And my soul is sick with sin,
And I scarce can see for weeping,
But the Lord will let me in.

SAINT STEPHEN.

O blessed martyr, dying for the Lord!
    We envy him the glory of his fate,
Though all that men most shrink from (burning word
    Of bitterest slander, hiss of scorn and hate,
More cruel than the heavy stones they cast),
Made storm about him as his spirit passed.

We envy him the peace that kept his heart
    In all the shock of that mad passion-war,—
We, whose watched doors of patience fly apart
    So often at temptation's lightest jar;—
The peace that made his countenance to shine
Like Moses', hearing mysteries divine.

Full of the perfect love he knelt to die!
    He prayed his enemies might be forgiven,
And from the height of that great ecstacy
    He looked in through the open gate of Heaven!
He saw the Lord! Pain o'er him had no power,
Entering to be with Christ forevermore.

The first to die for Jesus! Oh, how sweet
    To die for love of Jesus! This we say,
And straight toward Golgotha we turn our feet
    With faces like a flint; but on our way
We meet the little crosses we must take,
And bear upon our shoulder for His sake.

And so we shrink, and falter, and turn back,
    Or with complaints and murmurs take them up,
The small denials, neither scourge nor rack;—
    We sigh to sit with Ease and drink her cup,
And walk Sloth's level gardens;—we, who fain
The stature of Christ's martyrs would attain!

And can it be, dear Lord, that souls so weak,
    Remiss in watching, dastard in the fight,
Shall walk upon the eternal hills, and speak
    With Stephen, bearing palm and robed in white?
Ashamed, in tears, we come for help to Thee,
Triumphant Captain, Lord of victory!

STRANGE SURPRISES.

WHAT strange surprises meet us as we go !
   Extremes of joy and grief !
Unlooked-for partings full of wildest woe,
   Or fraught with rare relief !

Unlooked-for meetings, big with heavy fate,
   Changing us, evermore,
As, russet-clad, with Sorrow for our mate,
   We pace the desert-shore ;

Or, as we urge the swift-wheeled chariot on
   In Joy's mad carnival,
Throwing our roses out till all are gone,
   Unheeding where they fall.

Sometimes the strange surprise is heavenly gain ;
   Our scanty loaf we share
With some mean guest, and lo ! we entertain
   An angel unaware !

Or we go toying with the perfumed Hours
   Along Life's greenest lanes,—
A serpent darteth from a hedge of flowers
   And poisons all our veins!

Sometimes it is a curdling mystery;
   As one in woods of June
Findeth a corpse in that sweet nook where he
   Was wont to read at noon.

And oh! sometimes the sweet surprise is this,—
   Out in the dusky morn
Weeping our lost hope and our buried bliss'
   Most wretchedly forlorn,

We meet our dear dead Lord Himself and hear
   His kind voice call our name;
We touch His robe with fingers stiff and sere,
   Scorched with the furnace flame.

    *   *   *   *   *

I marvel what the strange surprise may be
   Across the roaring tide;
How many will come down to welcome me
   Of those I knew this side;

What holy mysteries will amaze my sight,
   Going alone away
Out of the starry glory of the night
   Into the perfect day!

BALLAD OF THE BOATS.

> AMONG the isles of the golden mist
>   I lived for many a year,
> And all that chanced unto me there
>   'T is well that ye should hear.
> —*Howitt.*

I walked along the river shore,
    And gathered greenwood moss and bells ;
And on the damp sand, o'er and o'er,
    I wrote my name with shining shells.
I played with wavelets, glad and free,
    When lo ! a little boat drew nigh
That swam the waters daintily ;
    Its flag was colored like the sky.

And as I watched the canvas swell,
    A boy I saw who seemed to me
Some spirit of a pearly shell,
    That saileth in the Indian Sea.

So gentle, delicate, and slight,
  I thought of fairy lily-bells;
His forehead had their charm of white,
  His eyes were violets of the dells.

His boat was heaped with heart's-ease, blent
  With blossoms rare from far-off bowers;
He passed so near me as he went
  He threw me handfuls of the flowers;
He passed so near me on the strand
  I reached my own and touched his hand.

"The boat," I said, "is small, and such
  As tempest-shock will rend apart";
But on my hand I kept the touch,
  And kept the flowers upon my heart;
And when he passed, with willow wand
  Wrote idle verses on the sand.

I loitered on the sylvan shore,
  Sweet flutings from the branches fell;
And all the while I hidden wore
  A heart's-ease from the pearly shell;

No other flower, in sun or shower,
   Was like to that in hue or smell.

*   *   *   *   *   *

A sweet surprise has starred my eyes,
   And stirred my cheek to tinge of dawn!
The pearly shell, I mind so well,
   Upon the woody shore is drawn!
The flag I knew, of heavenly blue,
   Is moving under boughs of green;
While wafts of song shake down the dew
   From homes that nestle there unseen.

The boy—his cheek is bronzed with noon,
   The beard is on his lip—and see!
Queen-roses of the gorgeous June,
   And myrtle spray, he offers me.
And while the sweet words stir his lip,
   "There's room, beloved, for thee and me,"
The little boat becomes a ship—
   A ship that bears me out to sea.

What though I leave the bowers behind,
　　And all the pretty wood-flowers now?
I ride the bounding waves and bind
　　The large white sea-pearls on my brow!
The wind that walks upon the brine
　　Breaks diamonds on the emerald floor!
And he who holds the helm is mine—
　　Forevermore—forevermore!

THE MERRY MAY WEATHER.

THERE are cooings, and flittings, and carols be-
    tween,
For the nest is the fairest that ever was seen,
And the loves are young and the leaves are green;
    And now 't is the merry May weather.

And the dandelion is scattered bold,
As a prodigal passing had dropped his gold;
And the apple-tree weareth the garland of old,
    And the willow her swaying feather.

The cattle call from the sunset lanes,
And lambs from the grassy slopes and plains;
And mark! for the joy of the dancing rains
    How the hills laugh out together!

But the winds of autumn will wail and sigh;
The hawk will scream in the stormy sky;
The festal garlands fall sere and dry,
    And the soft-eyed Loves be flying.

But not for the Loves that the May-time brings ;
For her that listens, or him that sings,
Or the little blue eggs that will wake with wings,
    Shall our hearts to-night be sighing.

For we know that their little ones all, and they,
May sing in the land of the rising day,
In the glorious islands far away,
    When the summer here is dying.

OUR MOTHER.

SHE was born in March, in the wintry March,
    When the cold wind shaking the northern larch
        Like a homeless ghost was grieving;
And the broidered lace, for the window's grace,
        Was the frost's fantastic weaving.

She should have been born on a winsome morn,
When the faint life stirred in the buried corn,
        When labor was song and beauty;
And dear mother Earth, through the children's mirth,
        Was doing her housewife duty.

Or she should have been born in the evening time,
When the marsh has a sound as of bells a-chime
        That ring for a bridal merry;
And the cool green blood is astir in the bud
        With promise of leaf and berry.

For her eyes are keeping a look of May,
Of violets, hid in the wood away,
    That whisper their sweet-lipped story ;
And her hair, in the time of the winter's rime,
    Is wearing its amber glory.

And her heart is a garden warm with spring,
Where the Loves and the Sympathies build and sing,
    Where the healing leaves are growing ;
And Labor and Skill their honey-cells fill
    In a clime no winter knowing.

LEFT BEHIND.

ANOTHER has gone through the evening gate
    That shuts in the golden west:
The shadows deepen, the hour is late,
And I sit here in the dark and wait
    My call as a wedding guest.

And I fondly think when the morn was here,
    And the trees were alive with May,
How friends were many and help was near,
And the hearts were strong where I leaned in fear;
    And life was a holiday.

How long it seems since the day began,
    And the hills were tipped with gold!
The feet now falter that fleetly ran,
And the hands that wrought what the brain might plan
    Are tremulous now and old.

LEFT BEHIND.

We hear the messenger's heavy tramp,
    As the pilgrims pass away,
All under the arches chill and damp,
With never a glimmer of torch or lamp,
    To the Sun of an endless day.

For, one by one, with their sins aneled,
    They answer the midnight call;
To the marvellous lore of the volumes sealed,
To the joy of the mysteries unrevealed,
    They pass through the dreary hall.

We see their foreheads light up with grace
    As they enter the farther door;
A flash of light from a shining place,
A look as of one who seeth the face
    Of Him who hath gone before.

I linger on by the lonesome gate
    Who leaned on the loving breast;
The shadows deepen, the hour is late,
And left behind in the dark I wait
    My call as a wedding guest.

OUR SISTER.

SHE came to us first when the rose was superb,
    In the freshness and beauty of June,
When the paly-green bloom of the grape gave perfume,
    And the birds sang the last summer's tune.

A frail little thing, like a bird of the spring
    That lieth all trembling and bare :
June led on the summer, the seasons went by,
    And another June came unaware ;
It changed into hazel her pansy-hued eyes,
    And deepened the gold of her hair.

Day called unto day, night answered to night,
    And the great heart of nature kept beating,
And June followed June like an exquisite tune
    That God never wearies repeating.

The summer rain fell, and the sunshine as well,
    And the night brought the freshness of dew,
Till our bud half apart showed the gold at its heart,
    And the lover-bee came there to woo.

'T is the June of her being, full, perfect and rare !
  'T is the June hastening on to July ;
The fulness of flower-time is filling the air,
  And the May-birds are still in the sky.
Who says that the tempest will fall unaware,.
  And the lightning flash down from on high ?

That the winter will come, when the birds shall be dumb,
  And the rose-branches frosty and bare ?
I thank Thee, my Father ! my heart is content,
  I know that Thou hast her in care ;
The winter may come, when the birds will be dumb,
  But never the night of despair.

THE MIDSUMMER CHILD.

THE web of her life took up its woof,
   And our hearts began to love her,
In the old gray home with the gambrel roof
   And the woodbine climbing over.

A broken chirp from the tree's repose
   Where the birds are lightly sleeping;
A waft of spice from the "red, red rose,"
   By the rustic gateway creeping.

Did the old-world fairies come and dance
   On the greensward of our dingle?
Or was it only the fire-flies' glance
   Where the brook and river mingle?

She came on the fairies' midsummer night,
   The child of the poet-fancies,
And the dark of her eyes holds an opal light,
   Like dew in the purple pansies.

But nothing had she of the out-of-tune
    Of an elf-child's incompleteness,
Our little queen-rose of the royal June,
    With her winsome human sweetness.

She was sent with the glory on her brow
    From the angels' perfect summer,
With the "red, red rose" we'll crown her now,
    Our old home's latest comer!

MEMORIES OF OUR FATHER.

THOU gavest thy father honor;—
   Such honor is due to thee;
For thou did'st teach by thy word and deed
   Us little ones on thy knee,
Better than aught in the schoolmen's creed,
   What the heavenly love might be.
From thy fatherly pity we well can guess
At the Lord's divinest tenderness.

O kindest heart, that never
   For bread gave any a stone!
Rousing in deep of the drowsy night
   For the restless little one,
To draw cool water from out the well,
Or the nursery legend belov'd to tell
   In thy patient, cheery tone.
Ah! few are they who have better shown
How the Heavenly Father tends His own!

MEMORIES OF OUR FATHER.

O memories old and fragrant,
　Of lessons better than play,
Out in the lane where the sweetbrier grew,
Down in the glen where the heron flew,
　Or in orchards sweet with May!
Lessons learned from our mother and thee
Of the building bird, the upholstering bee;
Of small, shy creatures that dwelt in the wood,
That burrowed the earth, or that swam the flood.

When the wild geese had flown southward,
　And the river in slumber lay,
There were Scripture stories before the fire
　At Saturday's set of day;
Or we went to the lands of our desire
　With the poets, far away;—
Saw lights and shadows of Scottish skies;
Or we dwelt with Milton in Paradise;
Or in Village Deserted with Goldsmith walked;
Or in copse and dingle with Cowper talked;
　Or the churchyard trod with Gray.
Then we sailed in the Mayflower back again,
To share in the pilgrim's joy and pain.

There were tales of the wild New England
    In a century gone by :
Tales of the days of terror and fear,
Of red men haunting the forest drear,
    And of deeds of valor high ;
Tales of the northern hunters bold ;
Tales of the diggers for buried gold ;
Tales of ancestral heroes gone ;
Of the stately days of Washington,
    And the young land's birthnight cry !
Or, further back, in the ages grand,
History and legend of mother-land.

O heart, to the Master loyal,
    To the truth forever true,—
Thou wroughtest good by a secret word
    And the great world never knew !
From thy prudent lips none ever heard
    Aught foolish, or harsh, or vile ;
Or the swelling words of vanity,
    Or the crafty words of guile ;
But oh ! the cheer of thy sympathy,
    And the comfort of thy smile !

Meek, and for evil returning good,
A son of the Lord's beatitude !
Thy record is kept by the Lord alone,
Blessed is he whom His lips shall own !

LU AND I.

THE spicy scent of the hemlock boughs!
    It is bringing my childhood back anew!
The fairy wood by the mottled rocks
    Where the speckled partridge flew,—
The rare green wood, where the hemlocks stood,
    And the one white birch tree grew!

And Lu and I are the owners twain
    Of the wealth of a dewy summer morn;
We hear the hymn of the early lark
    In the grassy meadows born,
And the whisper blithe of the mower's scythe,
    And the crows that clamor "corn."

We carry our porringers, Lu and I;
    For sweet cups hang on the raspberry spray;
We hear the voice of the cascade brook,—
    The truant is out at play;
But,—a solemn fate that will not wait,—
    The river goes on its way.

LU AND I.

The river, mysterious, grand, and calm,
    Goes voiceless down to the distant sea,
And Lu and I, on the mottled rocks,
    Know little where that may be;
We listen the lark, and we pull the bark
    From the graceful white birch tree.

We loiter and play like the truant brook;
    We learn where the housekeeping snails abide;
We shout as we dig up the waxen pipe
    That the brownies thought to hide;
And our footsteps scare the bonnie brown hare,
    And the lizard scarlet-pied.

The squirrels chatter and scream and laugh,
    The red-crest woodpecker taps the tree
As we fill our hands with the lady-fern
    And the blue wood-betony;
And all about are the hemlocks stout
    Brooding o'er Lu and me.

We know that our mother will stay for us
    In the home where the woodbine clambers wild,

And we loiter to smell at the clover flowers,
    And the red rose velvet-piled ;
She will wait all day with our Pansie gay,
    The winsome midsummer's child.

The truant brook to the river went ;
    The solemn river has found the sea ;
Our mother looks out from the woodbine home
    No longer for Lu and me ;
But, gone before, on the other shore
    She is waiting her darlings three.

OUR POSSESSION.

CROUCHED on a robe of bison
    Are little Lulie and I ;
We listen the wild New England tales
    Of a century gone by ;
And a spirit down the chimney wails,
    And the maple logs flame red,
And the sweetest child that ever was known,
The fairest, the dearest, and all our own,
    Is asleep in her baby bed.

This is the old home-picture,
    And the fire will always glow,
For Lulie and I will keep it bright
    However the winds may blow ;
For Lulie and I will watch it still
    Through the years that come and go ;
Though the sweetest baby that ever was known
Has long ago to a woman grown,
    And is dearer and sweeter so.

Though the ancient chimney now is gray,
    Though the father of our pride,
And the mother quick with her sympathy,
    In a fairer home abide,
Yet this is our sure possession,
    Whatever may still betide—
The memories dear of the hearts gone higher,
Of the love that lighted the household fire,
    And the wailing storm defied.

THE HOME VALLEY.

COME from the proud old city out,
　　From human din abroad,
Where the calm hills have walled about
　　This garden of the Lord ;

And thou shalt hear the hymn to God,
　　Ascending night and day,
That earth, baptized in holiest blood,
　　Pours from her heart alway ;

The choral concert in the trees ;
　　A sound of dropping fruit ;
The murmur of the honied bees
　　When noontide else were mute ;

The tune of insects in the grass ;
　　The tinkling of the rain ;
The breath of winds that lightly pass
　　Above the ripened grain ;

The voice of solemn waterfalls
    Low chanting like the sea ;
The brook-cascade, that laughs and calls
    And claps its hands for glee ;

The bugle-throated cock's disdain
    When morn doth earliest glow ;
The low of kine in grassy lane
    As evening paces slow,

And earth, from wood and garden soil,
    Gives tears and odors sweet,
Like weeping Mary pouring oil
    To bathe the Master's feet.

EMILY.

SHE says that she has listened as I sat and sung
    alone;
There were names that grew to music, but she never
    caught her own;
(They should have named her *Rose*, so rare-perfumed,
    richly blown :)
                      Sweet Emily!

Like the gorgeous eastern roses, delicious with the dew,
Eve's pitying angel planted, when she passed the gate-
    way through,
In the wilderness beyond, keeping Eden scent and
    hue,
                      Is she to me!

Like some rare and dainty poem I keep her in my
    heart,
And her face is like a treasure that I revel in apart;
And I tremble as I hold her, and tears begin to start;
                      I fear to stir!

The star 's too high for climbing, as many a poor heart
    knows,
The Persian poet's nightingale may sing about the
    rose,
And God's divinest poet, where the sapphire pavement
    glows,
    May sing of her!

VALLEY OF THE HEART'S-EASE.

LET me in the valley keep,
    Where the Master leads His sheep ;
Where the stillest waters flow ;
Where the heart's-ease loves to grow.

In the pastures of His choice,
Following His tender voice ;
Never questioning His will ;
Ever drawing closer still.

When the hills with tempest rock,
When the wolf is in the flock,
I so near Him shall have pressed
He will catch me to His breast.

Let me in His garden walk,
Where the ring-doves softly talk ;
Where He notes His sparrows small,
If they fly or if they fall ;

Where the lilies, low and sweet,
Fain would kiss His sacred feet,
Where the little violet
Spinneth not with toil or fret ;

Where the smiling of His face
Is the sunshine of the place ;—
Far from clamor, strife, and pride,
Let me here with Him abide.

THE POET'S FRIENDS.

THE robin sings in the elm ;
  The cattle stand beneath,
Sedate and grave, with great brown eyes,
  And fragrant meadow-breath.

They listen to the flattered bird,
  The wise-looking stupid things !
And they never understand a word
  Of all the robin sings.

(W. D. Howells, in *Atlantic Monthly.*)

THE "CATTLE" TO THE "POET."

HOW do *you* know what the cow may know,
    As under the tasselled bough she lies,
When the earth is abeat with the life below,
When the orient mornings redden and glow,
When the silent butterflies come and go,—
    The dreamy cow with the Juno eyes?

How do you know that she may not know
    That the meadow all over is lettered "love,"
Or hear the mystic syllable low
In the grasses' growth, and the water's flow?
How do you know that she may not know
    What the robin sings on the twig above?

"INASMUCH."

IN land as lovely as Eden,
    Homesick and heavy with pain,
I lay on my weary pillow,
    Conning the old refrain ;
" Lingering here, year added to year,
    What do I hope to gain ? "

" And oh ! " I cried, " for my mother,
    Gone to the palmy land !
Oh ! for the voice of another,
    Still on the sea-beat strand,
Soothing the pain of the burning brain
    With the touch of the loving hand !

" Oh ! to put off this garment !
    Oh ! to unloose the shoon !
Heaviness changed to pinions,
    Dissonance turned to tune !
Fresh as the fragrant morning,
    Bright as the burnished noon ! "

'T was thus I clamored, impatient,
   Beating the cage to be free ;
For I of the body was weary,
   And the body was weary of me !
While the birds of the blossoming South-land
   Were singing about me for glee !

'T was thus I clamored, impatient
   Of torture that never kills ;
And I longed for the blue-gray mountains ;
   I sighed for the bare brown hills ;
For the river brimming over
   From the lately loosened rills !

Where the pilgrim's " May-flower," trailing,
   Finds only its sweetheart mates,
And the pale blue star of Houston
   That smiles like a soul who waits.
Where fretted with frosty jewels
   The blades of the grass complain,
And the vexed crows bicker vainly,
   Seeking the unsown grain.

    *   *   *   *   *

"INASMUCH."

Violets came to my bedside—
   Violets purple and white—
Rare and sweet as a sonnet
   A seraph might stoop to write,
Hinting of mystic music
   Sung in the halls of light.

Smiling from mossy cushions,
   Wee things, daintily wrought,
That out of the loving heavens
   A message of cheer had caught,
Comfort and blessing brought me
   Uttered in fragrant thought!

Love in the land of strangers,
   (Thus doth the Lord rebuke!)
Freighted the fairy basket
   Out of an Eden nook!
The kindness done to Thy "little one"
   Oh! note in Thy golden book!

The violets rest in my Bible—
   Scentless, withered and dry,

Over the words of comfort,
　　The sayings of Christ, they lie;
Over the words of promise
　　Whose sweetness never will die!

THE HEART'S COMPLAINT.

ANSWERED my heart as I sat alone
   And looked at the fading trees,—
"Shall the beggar, begging before the throne,
   Not take what the King shall please?"
For I heard her secretly making moan,
   "There were bonnier days than these":

"Days when the robin was singing," she said,
   "When the lilac wore its plume,
When the naked apple-tree over my head
   Was a bright bouquet of bloom,—
The bridal bower of the building bird,
   And the small bee's banqueting-room;

"When the summers were long and the winters fair;
   When the snow was a pearly rain;
And my mother, so young and debonair,
   Was soothing my lightest pain,
And I played with the curls of her amber hair
   As I never shall play again.

"My grandmother, dear as dear could be,
  Sat in her straight-backed chair,
Crooning an ancient ballad to me,
  Or a legend quaint and rare;—
Days that will never return," said she,
  "Whatever the future bear."

Then I answered back with a sharp rebuke;—
  "O blind and unthankful one!
For the violets still in the garden nook
  That smile to the autumn's sun;
For the birds that still by the singing brook
  Stay on when the summer is done;

"For the love that lingers—the rare old wine!
  For the sweet surprise, and dear,
Of the young fresh hearts that are born to thine
  In the waning of thy year;
For the tender touch of a Hand divine—
  Hast naught but a bitter tear?

"What knowest thou of the cycles grand
  In the vast eternity?

THE HEART'S COMPLAINT.

Or what may be in another land
   Just over the narrow sea?
Who says that the missing voice and hand
   Shall never return to thee?

" Hast thou forgotten whose name is Love?
   And that only thine unbelief,
That scorneth the Lamb and scareth the Dove,
   Can give thee to hopeless grief?
Hast thou forgotten who sits above,
   In this time of the falling leaf?

" The Great and the Wise! He shares with none
   The secret of His decrees!
The Good and the Gracious! in love alone
   He guideth our destinies!
Shall the beggar, begging before the throne,
   Not take what the King shall please?"

THE DREAM.

THE day was drear, the hills about
  Were garmented with mists and rains;
Gray was our little world without,
  Seen through the narrow window-panes.

Within was ruddy warmth and cheer;
  The jovial flame that leaps and falls,
From out the chimney quaint and queer,
  Laughed on the homely kitchen walls.

My mother in the corner sat
  And mended garments silently,
While opposite, the cheery cat
  Hummed loud a household melody.

And guests were there, polite and learned;
  But he and I, the blaze before,
Unheeding, sat and eager turned
  A curious volume o'er and o'er.

THE DREAM.

The golden leaves were clasped with gold;
  It was a dainty book and rare;
Illuminations strange and old
  Flashed out upon us here and there.

And on each amber-tinted leaf
  A poet spake of joy and pain,
Of blessedness that comes from grief,
  In music-words that thrilled the brain.

'T was but a foolish dream, I know,
  For, voyaging on unknown seas,
He passed before me, long ago,
  Into the land of mysteries.

Yet, cycles hence—who can discern?
  Perhaps, safe housed from stormy weather,
It may fall out that we shall turn
  The leaves of some strange lore together.

DEAR EMILY.

I DREAMED of thee, my darling,
    With eyes of the antelope,
And laugh of the tinkling river
    That falls from the Alpine slope.

We stood in the garden-meadow
    Where the clover reached our knees,
And the kingcups shook with laughter
    At the pranks of the frolic breeze.

We spoke of thy far-off hero
    Who went at the bugle's call;
Who hath taken *his* commission
    From the Captain over all.

We sat at the festal table;
    We talked in the summer-bower;
In the sunshine of thy beauty
    A day was a passing hour.

But I felt over brain and spirit
   The invalid languor creep,
And kissing my beautiful darling
   I sank on my couch asleep.

The crimson wine of the sunset
   Was poured in the limpid stream,
When I woke and sought thee, Emmie,
   (I fancied this in my dream);

But the shrieking horse of iron,
   Like a fate that hated me,
Had whirled thee over the mountains
   To thy home beside the sea.

And I broke into passionate crying,—
   "O cruel and bitter fate!
Wherever she stays is Eden,
   And I am outside the gate!"

Awaked by my watching angel
   To the calm of the golden morn,
I said "I am only dreaming,"
   And I laughed my tears to scorn.

Ah! so we dream in our darkness!
    We are blessed and we repine;
We break into clamorous crying,
    And our pillows are wet with brine.

O Lover, who trod our valley!
    So grant us—the gift is thine—
To wake from the longing and weeping
    Where the morning is divine!

ROSSY.

INTO this life of death and pain,
    Into this world of strife and scorn,—
Where rude feet crush the springing grain,
Where white flowers catch a crimson rain,—
    I thank the dear Lord *she* was born.

She's like the snow on Lebanon
    To valleys lying all athirst;
She's like the breeze from ocean won;
She's like the frost, heaven-sent, upon
    Some wretched land a plague has curst.

She's like a lily of the pool
    To one whose brows with fever ache,—
So dainty-pure, and white, and cool,
So of a subtle sweetness full,—
    The chaste nymph of the limpid lake.

I sit by her and touch her dress
   With fingers tremulous and faint ;
Her presence charms my heart's distress,
Her very voice is a caress,
   Her eyes are sweet eyes of a saint.

There 's strength and healing in her touch ;
   There 's hope and comfort in her smile ;
Her smile, so like the smile of such
As in the furnace, suffering much,
   Have seen the face of Christ the while.

Into this life where brows must ache,
   Wearing the willow-weed forlorn,
Where trusted staves are reeds that break,
Where lush flowers hide the coiling snake,—
   I thank the dear Lord *she* was born.

   Bring her the violet tri-hued,
      The cheeriest flower that blows ;
   Lay on the green turf over her head
      The dear old cinnamon rose.

ROSSY.

A handful of apple-blossoms,
   With childhood's memories fraught;
Bring velvet pansies, purple and gold,
   Each one holding a thought.

Who knows but the soul of the roses
   . That grew by the farm-house door,
The subtle life in the violet's heart,
   Will whisper to her once more?

She hath gathered the leaf of healing,
   And the fruit that maketh wise;
Can the flowers be more divine than ours,
   In her walks in Paradise?

'Mid the fragrance of its lilies
   Does her heart go back—who knows?
To the violets and the apple-bloom,
   And the dear old cinnamon rose?

MARY.

SHE was my May when my winter had come,
Bringing back music to forests all dumb!
Delicate wild-wood anemone, she!
Lily-bell, swinging out fragrance for me!

Crystal, as pure and transparent as light!
Moonbeam, delicious, that comforts the night—
Calming and cooling, with beauty divine,
Earth overcome with the noon's ruddy wine.

Shut with the few on the tempest-tossed deck—
All the world outward a blank and a wreck,
Sailing the sea of a desolate grief,
She was my dove with the green olive leaf.

'T was Mary who cradled our Lord on her breast;
A Mary who loved Him and pleased Him the best;
A Mary it was who anointed His head;
A Mary who welcomed Him first from the dead.

MARY.

Thank God! with the sorrow of wearisome years,
He sendeth us Marys to wipe off our tears,
To touch the sick brain with His infinite calm,
To bind up the crucified heart with His balm.

IN MEMORY OF L. J. R.

IF Faith came not to hold our hand
   How weary we should be,
Wandering along the lonesome strand
   That bounds the narrow sea,
While one by one our best beloved
   Pass o'er, dear Lord, to Thee.

She walks with us and holds our hand,
   Her eyes are angel's eyes;
She walks with us across the sand,
   Sweet Faith, from out the skies!
Wearing a rose upon her breast
   That smells of Paradise.

"O God! that he should pass away,
   So far from us who love him,
Wasting with hot pain day by day,
   And none to watch above him.
No tender hands his eyes to close,
   No time for farewell-taking!"

IN MEMORY OF L. J. R.

So said a foolish heart that knows
    The trick of secret aching.
" To think, of all he loved, that none
    Were busy by his pillow,
Or watched him as he stepped alone
    Upon the ice-cold billow ! "

But Faith, who knows what words of cheer
    Will keep our hearts from breaking,
Tells how the river, crystal clear,
    The fever-thirst is slaking ;
With more than mother's care and thought
    The Healer, Christ, stood by him,
One pang too many, suffering not,
    In all his pain, to try him !

Tells how, upon the brow so dear,
    Christ's hand stilled all the throbbing :—
O then the sound that caught his ear
    Was not the sound of sobbing !
For with the love that maketh bold,
    He left the shore forever,
And glorious spirits, manifold,
    Walked with him o'er the river !

THE DEAR ONE DEAD.

Sometimes I am full of sorrow
   When I think of the dear one dead;—
How we never shall listen at morn or eve
   For the sound of his gentle tread;
How he lay with the wasting fever-pain,
   And the *stranger* was by his bed.

How we walk no more, as we walked of yore,
   When the dew begins to fall;
Nor watch with him at the western door
   For the sunset's carnival;
Like a sharp sword striketh the "Nevermore"
   That answers the heart's wild call!

Sometimes I am full of triumph
   As I think of the early dead;—
How he walks beneath the immortal trees
   With the glory 'round his head;
How his food is the feast of the eucharist,
   And Christ is breaking the bread!

How he talks with high archangels ;
   And wings to his wish are given ;
And he floats in the calm of a perfect love
   In the radiance we call heaven ;
And every day is a Sabbath day,
   And the light is the light of seven !

THE BROKEN SPELL.

WITH the roses dropping earthward,
    In some year departed long,
From a brain that throbbed too wildly
    Died the glorious sense of song.

Still the summer winds went talking,
    Among the voiceless leaves;
Birds swung upon the branches;
    The reapers bound the sheaves;
And the busy mother-swallows
    Fed their young beneath the eaves.

The brown brook wandered singing
    A low and sweet lament;
Along the purple mountains
    The shadows came and went;
And above the pilgrim-river
    The blue sky stretched its tent.

THE BROKEN SPELL.

The sheen was there, and the beauty,
   But the brain was cold and numb;
The high stars moved to music,
   But the soul was deaf and dumb,
And the olden spell of August
   To the poet would not come.

Then the grand magician, Winter,
   Strove to loose the fettered tongue;
How the child-heart leaped to greet him
   When the buried years were young!
For the glory that he showed her
   No poet ever sung!

The forests took regalia
   That shamed the gifts of June;
They wore diamonds for the morning,
   And opals for the noon;
They wore rubies for the sunset,
   And pearls beneath the moon!

The umbered ferns and grasses
   Peeped through broideries of lace,

The brown brook, cased in crystal,
    Sung softly in its place,
As one hides a happy secret
    With a too transparent face.

O'er the slopes of molten silver,
    Through the dim, mysterious dells,
Past the marbled cascade's turrets,
    Glistening bright in lonesome fells,
There was flying in the moonlight
    To the merry rhyme of bells.

The sheen was there, and the beauty,
    But the brain was still and numb;
The high stars moved to music,
    But the soul was deaf and dumb,
And the olden spell of Winter
    To the poet would not come.

Beneath the starry splendor,
    Or the beauty of the morn,
She saw but dusky shadow—
    And 't was thus she sung forlorn,

THE BROKEN SPELL.

Like the nightingale, complaining,
  With her breast against the thorn :

  "The pulse is away
  From the painted clay,
And the dull eyes only stare ;
  Here 's the cup, here 's the vine,
  But the rare old wine,
Will it ever again be there ?

  "Should the whole broad earth
  Forego its mirth
For a grave on the sunny slope?
  Should the starry belt
  From the firmament melt
Like the light of a dying hope ?

  "Should the valleys mourn
  That a saint is borne
To the shining hills of home ? "
  She reasoned well,
  But the olden spell
To the poet would not come.

"What matter?" I said,
"*Christ* is not dead!
He can make the sick soul strong!
Thou yet shalt stand
In the pleasant land,
And join in the infinite song!"

TO WHAT SHALL I LIKEN HER?

TO what shall I liken this love of mine?
   To what shall I liken her?
She is a sunny and fruited vine,
Hinting a promise of purple wine,
Whose delicate tendrils cling and twine
   Over a desolate fir.

What is this love of mine to me?
   To what shall I liken her?
She is a blush-rose sweet to see
To the nightingale, or the beggar-bee;
A sensitive plant, an aspen-tree,
Thrilling and sighing with sympathy,
   If a sad wind do but stir.

To what shall I liken my love, I pray?
   To what shall I liken her?
She is a bountiful summer day,
Golden and emerald, grave and gay,
Keeping the spring-time roundelay,

But crowned with her harvests, a queen alway;
Dearer to me than the frolicsome May,
   With its wings of gossamer.

To what shall I liken my love again?
   To what shall I liken her?
To the summer day with its golden grain?
To the harvest waiting the empty wain?
To the aspen stirred with another's pain?
To the rose that opes to the nightingale's strain?
To the vine, distilling the sun and the rain
In its many alembics, rich in stain,
   Smelling of spice and myrrh?

She is an angel Christ hath sent—
   Thus will I liken her!
When the moon from my firmament suddenly went,
And the household lamp from my dreary tent,
And the sky like sackcloth over me bent,
And I mused, in the dark, what the Father meant—
Lo! over my head was the blackness rent,
And there came from the glory excellent
A message of comfort, of love unspent!
   And she was the messenger!

PRINCESS AND POET.

LIKE silence fell the moonlight's sheen
    At the fairies' trysting hour,
And it touched the gems on the shaded green,
    And over the trembling flower ;

When a strain of music stole across
    To the queen-rose, royal-bright,
And the little white violets in the grass
    Awoke in a rare delight.

'T was not the pipe of Pan they heard,
    Nor the serenade of fay ;—
But the passionate heart of a poor brown bird
    Was pouring its roundelay

To the worshipped rose, the peerless rose,
    With the diamond on her breast,
With a fragrant soul that the poet knows
    In Araby, the blest !

They had told her of the eagle's mein,
    Of his fiery heart and eye :
Oh, who should match the garden-queen
    But the monarch of the sky ?

But she listened the loving serenade,—
    It was sweet as an eastern tale,—
And her royal heart of fire was swayed
    To the little brown nightingale !

1776.

THE red-coats merrily crossed the sea,
    And the hills cried out in wonder
At the beat of drum, at the bugle's glee,
    And the cannon's brazen thunder.

They had sent their threats and their taunts before,
    For their pride would take no warning;
And they sailed the sea and they trod the shore
    Like Lucifer, son of the morning!

O who so rare in their trappings brave,
    Their golden and scarlet splendor!
They came the poor and the weak to enslave;
    For them there was no defender!

Their coats were ragged, their feet were bare,
    But their will was tempered iron!
The tyrants plucked at a silken hair,
    But they wakened a sleeping lion!

They made burlesque of Jonathan's words,
    And they called him "boor" and "noodle";
But their officers brave gave up their swords
    To the tune of Yankee Doodle!

'T was a long and dreary and pitiless night,
    But there came a glorious dawning;
And the proud ones fell from their lofty height
    Like Lucifer, son of the morning.

THE FALSE SECRET.

'TWAS the thistle that told the yellow-bird,
   And the yellow-bird told the bee;
And the gossip wind, that overheard,
   Went telling the willow-tree.
And that is the way that the little tree-frog
   Is supposed to know it all;
He told his cousins that lived in a bog,
   And they croaked to the rushes tall;
They whispered the reptiles that live in the mud,
   And wriggle and creep and crawl,
To tell the mosquitoes that feast on blood—
   That a star was seen to fall.

But the lilies knew that it could not be true,
   The lilies that looked on high;
And the waters blue, where the lilies grew;
   Not so the little fire-fly;
He met his friends where the garden ends
   And the low marsh-meadows lie;

They said it was sad as sad could be
  That a star must fall and die,
And the goblin meteors danced with glee ;—
  But the star is still in the sky !

THE BENEDICTION.

'TWAS June in all the land,
    And life went merrily,
With buds of rose for every hand
    And birds on every tree ;
But half distraught with pain I thought
    That there was none for me.

When evening's purple gloom
    Wrapt all the valley o'er,
Fair gentle fingers to my room
    A fragrant rose-branch bore ;
I breathed perfume, I seized the bloom
    For which my heart was sore.

A thorn went through my hand !
    There showed no crimson stain,
But left a wound none understand
    The art to heal again ;
And no one knows but that false rose
    And I, who feel the pain.

I was as one forlorn
   And lost in murky wood,
Who sees, at last, the crescent horn
   On forehead of the good
Fair huntress-maid, light up the glade,
   And joy thrills all his blood!

And rushing to her side
   With all too eager feet,
And reaching forth to grasp his guide
   With earnestness unmeet—
For fair Dian, lo! jeering Pan
   His startled gaze doth greet!

And so my terror bore
   My feet to tangled mesh;
But Christ, my Lord, whose wounds were more
   Than rose-thorns in the flesh,
Came at my cry, and tenderly
   Upon my head afresh

His benediction laid;—
   O that dear hand of His!

THE BENEDICTION.

My foolish heart, no more afraid,
 The sorrow would not miss,
The cruel thorn, the jeering scorn,
 So she might keep but this!

OUT IN THE WILDERNESS.

ONCE was treading, wearily, alone,
   A frightful wilderness.   The starless night
Hung round me like the blackness of a pall.
I heard the fearful cry of evil beasts ;
I saw at intervals the lightning play—
A fiery snake that lighted up the dark—
Above an endless pit that yawned for me.
I called on names beloved : the lonesome wood
Sent back my cry.   A wail was on the wind,
And phantoms strange seemed beckoning me below.

Where, then, was He whose name the demons fear ?
I could not find *my Lord*.   A storm arose—
A storm which shook the earth beneath my feet,
And rent in twain the old gigantic trees ;
And on the howling wind there seemed to ride
The fiendish forms that mock and taunt and sneer :
None else replied. Where, then, was Christ, the Lord ?

Was He no more, that hell kept carnival ?
I called aloud, " I trust though Thou dost slay :
Shine on my path, O Bright and Morning Star ! "

My feet beside the pit began to slide ;
When, from above, a hand, a powerful hand,
Held me, and drew me back, and led me on.
Above the wilderness there broke a light,—
A clear soft dawning, as of dewy day ;
A light like to the smile of one beloved,
Who loves us without stint. Then music fell :
Was it the flutings of the greenwood birds,
Or half-caught hymnings sliding down from heaven ?
And still the heart of love and arm of strength
Bear me along the brightening wilderness.

  Let not go thy trust, poor soul !
   With benumbèd hands
  Hold where crested billows roll
   Over sinking sands.
  Hold the cord thrown out to thee,—
   Slender thread of hope :

At the far extremity
    It becomes a rope.

Lo ! along the electric line
    More and more will flow
Pulsings from a hand divine
    That will not let thee go.
Cling, though it may seem to thee
    But a thread of hope:
At the far extremity
    Jesus holds the rope.

Seas and tempest hear His voice ;
    He has walked the wave :
Fear not, therefore, but rejoice,
    Jesus loves to save.
Cling, though it may seem to thee
    But a thread of hope :
At the far extremity
    Jesus holds the rope.

CHRIST IS IN THE UNIVERSE.

RESTLESS heart, that, worn with pain,
    Dost thy bitter griefs rehearse,
Cease to murmur and complain :
    Christ is in the universe !

Pilgrim, footsore, weak and poor,
    Bearing neither scrip nor purse,
Hope, and cheerfully endure :
    Christ is in the universe !

Wretched one, with conscience weighed
    Heavily with secret curse,
Heavenward turn and cry for aid :
    Christ is in the universe !

Soul in darkness, wrestling sore,
    Doubts of Him forbear to nurse,
Knock and seek, and ne'er give o'er :
    Christ is in the universe !

Anxious one, perturbed, distressed,
Evermore foreboding worse,
Comfort thee in thy unrest :
Christ is in the universe !

THE BELOVED STRANGER.

THE stranger came across the sea
    And sat beside our hearth;
Without, the world was wintry gray;
She brought a dream of English May,
Of English larks at early day,
    The English cuckoo's mirth.

She brought the English robin's note,
    The English primrose pale;
We saw within our little room
The hawthorn hedges all in bloom,
We smelt the violet's perfume,
    We heard the nightingale.

Around the English Christmas board
    We sit in merry thought;
We walk with her the storied land,
We tread cathedrals vast and grand,
And mystic symbols understand,
    Where the dead ages wrought.

O land, revered from childhood up,
   Whose poets sang for me,—
Shall e'er for me the dream come true
To wet my foot in English dew,
And hear thy larks sing in the blue,
   O land beyond the sea?

Shall ever side by side with thee,
   Dear stranger God did send,
Behold the haunts of old renown
And walk the streets of London town,
E'er all our years of earth be flown,
   O precious English friend?

However this may be, we know
   Our city out of sight
Shall satisfy our whole desire
When He to whom our hearts aspire
Himself shall bid us come up higher
   And walk with Him in white!

THE YOUNG MOTHER.

TINY shoes of red morocco
   Lie upon the chamber floor;
Merry eyes of sweetest sapphire
   Gayly peep within the door.

Oh how often, careless-hearted,
   Leaned I by this window frame;
Half a score of summers younger,
   Wearing still my father's name.

Blossoms lie, like gleams of moonlight,
   On the tops of chestnut trees;
To the red lips of the clover
   Go the bandit humble-bees.

Trembling branches dimly curtain
   Now, as then, my window scene;
Now, as then, a dryad trilleth
   Deep within the heart of green.

Here the soft wind came to kiss me
   In the balmy blossom time ;
Here I prayed with tears of anguish ;
   Here I wrote my girlish rhyme.

Here my lover's words of promise
   Made the whole world sweet and true ;
Now the tiny shape beside me
   Wears his gentle eyes of blue.

Curls of blonde about her forehead,
   One white pearl-tooth in her mouth ;
Sweeter she than buds of roses
   Opening in the spicy south !

Lo ! I bring that Thou mayst touch her
   This young child Thou gavest me !
Master, Lord, Thy hand of blessing
   Lay upon her tenderly !

WATCHING MOTHER.

THE heavy night is retiring,
    While alone the vigil I keep;—
For I see not the sentinel angel
    That watches the child asleep,
And the eyes of my faith are weaker
    And dimmer than those that weep.

In fear and distrust, in the noonday,
    I 've groped where the blind doubters go;
But O, when the tempest arises,
    My Saviour, Thy Godhead I know:
My soul in a moment is reaching
    To Thee, from the billows of woe.

I think of Thy mission of mercy;
    Remember Thy blood that was spilt;
Thy touch on the pulses of fever;
    Thy pardon to penitent guilt;
No longer I doubt Thee all-potent,—
    I know that Thou canst if Thou wilt.

The heavy night is retiring ;
   The sick child still slumbereth on ;
Oh, how will it be in the morning ?
   Oh, how when the sunset has gone ?
My heart, that is trembling and fainting,
   Doth cling to Thee, waiting for dawn.

I think how she lay in my bosom
   That sweet Sabbath morning in May,
And opened her eyes full of wonder,
   Her violet eyes to the day,
As giving her back with thanksgiving
   Her father knelt by us to pray.

Two Mays, with their lilies and roses,
   Have passed since that morning so fair ;
And now, in the time of the autumn,
   The dark of my sorrow and care,
My lips, that are pallid and trembling,
   Again take the words of his prayer ;—

" This great and new gift of Thy goodness
   We joyfully give back to Thee !

Thy precious possession, O Saviour,
    Forever Thine own let her be!
Whenever Thy love shall require her
    No right to withhold her have we.

"And this shall be now our petition :—
    Oh make her Thy covenant child!
In the mazes and by-ways of pleasure
    Oh ne'er let her feet be beguiled!
Oh give her Thy spirit in fulness,—
    Or take her ere sin has defiled!"

THE DEDICATION OF THE BABY.

GOD keep the baby of our love !
   We bring the child to Thee
Sealed with the holy Name of names
   Forever more to be !
God keep the forehead pure and frank,
   That ever there be seen
The token-cross, the soldier-sign,
   The badge of Constantine.

God keep the eyes—each one a dove,
   A violet-tinted dove—
That they may watch the Master's will
   As angels do above ;
That they, beholding vanity,
   Like doves may quickly fly,—
The happy eyes of those whose tears
   The Lord Himself will dry.

God keep the ears, the pearly doors
   That open to the soul,

THE DEDICATION OF THE BABY.

Attuned to hear the singing stars
    As 'round the throne they roll ;
Keep from the noise of clashing strife,
    The wily lure of wrong,
Temptation's whisper in the dark,
    The painted syren's song!
Teach them to hear, though ne'er so low,
    The call, "This is the way,"
And recognize in holy hush
    What heavenly watchers say!

God keep the lips, the budding lips
    With May all fragrant fair,
And when they learn the speech of men
    God guide the words they bear!
God keep them still from lying breath,
    From hot and hasty word,
From Judas' kiss, from Peter's oath,
    Denying Christ the Lord!
God keep the brain, the busy brain
    Where living thoughts shall glow,
From malice's plot, from passion's whirl,
    From madness' overthrow!

God watch and teach it still alway
    To know His loving hand,
And every message of His will
    Be quick to understand!

God keep the hands, the little hands,
    Twin roses pinky white,
That in His vineyard they may plant
    And prune and cull aright;
And in the kingdom that is Christ's
    Upbuild with loving skill;
From stain like Cain's, from Balaam's bribe,
    Preserve them spotless still!
From feverish clutch of glory's wreath,
    From greedy grasp of gold,
From tyrant work, from traitor deed,
    These little hands withhold!

God keep the feet, the dainty feet,
    That they may never stray,
But walking in the narrow path
    May find the shining way.
That, shod with gospel shoon of peace,

Swift flying they shall go
To carry tidings glad to those
   Who sit benumbed with woe ;
And, saved the serpent's poisoned fang,
   The roaring lion's den,
Shall pass through gate of pearl and tread
   The crystal street !   Amen !

MOTHER'S SONG.

JESUS is the Gardener,
   We are but the flowers;
If He prune the branches,
   If He bring the showers,
How should we rebuke Him?
   Is the garden ours?

If He pluck a lily,
   Joying in its white;
If He choose a rosebud
   For His own delight;
If He take it from us,
   Has He not the right?

Jesus is the Shepherd;
   If a lamb He bear
Unto higher pasture,
   Into purer air,
Should the flock that missed it
   Vex itself with care?

There the little lambkin
  Nothing shall distress;
There no cold shall chill it,
  There no heat oppress;
There no wolf shall enter
  Wearing shepherd's dress.

After snow the summer;
  Rainbow after rain;
Weeping but endureth
  With the night's short pain;
When the morning breaketh
  Joy will come again.

In the garden yonder,
  Eden of the blest,
We shall find the blossoms
  We have loved the best;
We shall find our lambkins
  Safe on Jesus' breast.

FAIRY MAY.

TO MY FRIEND, S. N. L.

WHY are such fair creations wrought,
   Perfect with God's divinest thought,
And yet so frail they turn to nought
    'Neath eyes that hold them dear?
His poet hand the rose hath made,
The tulip royally arrayed,—
Why doth He cause them thus to fade
    So early in the year?

And why hath vanished from our sight
Thy little lily, dainty white,
Like sunshine sliding into night
    In early morning hours?
A singing bird of budding spring!
A butterfly upon the wing!
The lightest, fleetest, fairy thing
    That ever danced o'er flowers!

FAIRY MAY.

Dear friend, my heart and eyes o'erflow ;
Well I remember, long ago,
When all my wine of life ran low,
   How thou didst comfort me !
And now thy turn has come to weep,
And thou, like me, hast laid asleep
A loved form for the earth to keep,
   Thus would I comfort thee.

Thy little one with flying feet
Shall never come thy steps to meet
In early garden-walk or street,
   An airy blossom sprite.
But well the skilful chemist knows
The subtle soul within the rose,
And 'neath his hand immortal grows
   The perfume of delight.

So e'en the fragile outward form
That broke, a white rose in the storm,
E'en that, in May times sweet and warm
   In fragrant shapes shall rise.

But she, herself, doth sing and play
In gardens beautiful as day,
And Christ will never say her nay
   In all His Paradise.

And when thy mansion, crystal bright,
With gold and precious stones bedight,
That now is building out of sight,
   Shall be complete for thee,
Shall not her swift feet through the door
As many and many a time before,
Her lips with music rippling o'er,
   Thy Heavenly welcome be?

LITTLE JULIA.

INSCRIBED TO MRS. JULIA P. BALLARD.

SWEET child whom the Lord hath ransomed
   Forever from sorrow and strife,
Already hast thou begun to know
   The power of an endless life!

Gone in the early morning
   To the land of song and love!
It is not for *thee* that our hearts are sore,
   O little white-pinioned dove!

'T is not for *thee* that our singing
   Is choked with the sobs of pain,
O lamb that the Shepherd has folded safe
   Away from the pitiless rain!

But oh! the heart of the mother
   That is yearning and aching so!
O loving Christ, who looked from the cross
   On the mother who stood below!

O loving and pitying Jesus,
  Whose heart with our grief is torn !—
Who givest more than Thou takest away
  When Thou comfortest those who mourn,

Oh, come with Thy large compassion
  To the home that misses her face !
With the fresh sweet gift of Thy wonderful love
  Come *Thou* to the empty place.

LITTLE WILLIE.

I HEARD the voice of an angel
    That chanted sweet and low:
" O fond pale mother, with cheek so wet,
    If thou could'st only know!
Thy son died on thy bosom,
    And his hands were pure from sin;
I carried him up to the temple above
    The new song to begin,—
I carried him up to the fold of love,
    And the Shepherd took him in.
On the ladder that reaches from heaven to earth
    Unseen I come and go,
And I hear the cry of mothers who weep
    For their sons who died—not so!"

THE BEREAVED MOTHER.

FOR MRS. A. R. H.

I AM thinking of the city
    Where Thy chosen walk in white;
Where Thou keepest, Lord of glory,
    Thy jewels in Thy sight.
I hear the choral singing;
    And the trust that he is there,
Whose smile has left our household,
    Lifts my heart from its despair.

The loved one of his sisters,
    We were proud to call him ours!
He came and went among them
    Like sunshine to the flowers,
Like rainbow after tempest
    Across the mountain flung,
Like a brave and flashing brooklet
    That laughs the hills among.

THE BEREAVED MOTHER.

As one within a garden,
   On a morn without a cloud,
I worshipped 'mong my blossoms,
   A mother glad and proud,—
My roses full of perfume,
   My young trees full of strength;
But the lightning and the whirlwind
   Have found me out at length.

And yet not so, my Father!
   I say not so; I see
Thy hand of love transplanting
   My beautiful young tree!
I brought him to Thee, Saviour,
   When his life was ebbing out
And my heart was almost breaking
   With the anguish and the doubt.

And I said with bitter weeping:
   "O ever-present One!
Like the mothers of Judæa,
   At thy feet I lay my son.

Thy house has many mansions,—
    Is there not for *him* a place?
Oh, clothe him for Thy presence,
    And let him see Thy face!

"He gave his parents honor,
    He was subject to our word;
Oh, let his days be lengthened
    In the Canaan of our Lord,
In the country over Jordan
    Where the living waters flow!—
To Thy wounded feet I'm clinging,
    I cannot let Thee go!"

I knew I was not worthy,
    But in His glorious name
Who wore our flesh unspotted
    With clinging faith I came;
I plead His tears of sorrow
    And the precious blood He spilt,
And I surely heard His answer,
    "Be it even as thou wilt."

THE SLAVE MOTHER.

CHARLOTTE PILES.

SISTERS with the heart of Martha
   Going forth the Lord to meet,
With the love of blessed Mary
   Pouring oil upon His feet,
Have you heard it? do you know it?
   Lo, our Lord is in the street!

Loving sisters, ye are many;
   How your hearts would throb to know
That along our pleasant city,
   Just released from slavery's woe,
Hungry, thirsting, faint, and needy,
   Christ with weary feet doth go.
Oh, we should not dare to say it
   But Himself hath told us so!

Oh, to give our roof for shelter!
   Oh, to share with Him our bread!
Like the blest Judean woman
   Bathe His feet, anoint His head!

But He counteth every kindness
   (We remember He hath said)
To the least of these, His children,
   As 't were done to Him instead.

One of these, His precious members,
   Pauseth at your door to-day,
With the brave heart of a mother
   Bearing up the shattered clay,
Black and poor, despised and lowly,
   For your pity come to pray;
Humbly suing in her sorrow,
   Sure you will not say her Nay.
Thus disguised it is the Master
   That you lightly send away.

Done to Thee, wilt Thou esteem it?
   O our Saviour, done to Thee!
When life's burdens grow too heavy
   This shall our rejoicing be,
Thou hast said it, we believe it,
   "Ye have done it unto Me."

THE SAVIOUR TO THE SORROWFUL SOUL.

LEAN on My breast, belovèd,
   Be comforted in Me,
Within thy Father's palace
   There is a place for thee.

Do I not feel thy sorrow?
   Have I not suffered too?
My arm is strong to bear thee
   The billowy waters through.

Lean on My arm, belovèd,
   And venture on the sea;
Fear not, for I have called thee;
   I'll walk the waves with thee.

Poor soul, why dost thou tremble?
   All worketh for thy good;
Do I not love thee better
   Than father, mother could?

Look to the Face that leaneth
   Thy troubled soul above,
And call me Friend and Brother,
   Thy Saviour and thy Love.

Trust Me, I will not leave thee;
   As they who went before,
So thou shalt reach in safety
   The green and sheltered shore.

Beside the peaceful river
   Thy loved ones thou shalt see;
Among the "many mansions"
   There is a place for thee.

THE UNSEEN KINGDOM.

DANIEL ii, 44; LUKE xvii, 20.

THE gifted tell, in song and history,
    How went the game of nations ages gone;
Who lost, who won, as crowned ones played at war.

They tell us how Assyria's glory waned,
How Persia found decay, how Egypt fell,
How Greece forgot her valor, and how Rome
Became as iron mix'd with miry clay.

Keen men look through the riot, eagle-eyed,
And to the surface-gazers bare the springs,
The secret, strong, electric springs that move
The mad machinery that makes the earth
In all her nerves to tremble, and the thrones,
The ancient principalities and powers,
The cherished institutions, old as sin,
To fall like Lucifer.

They show us these,
And yet, and yet they do not see His hand,
The humblest 'mong the children marks so well ;
The Hand Omnipotent, that works through all,
And ever for that kingdom without end
He hath set up on earth.

The years move on,
And then the centuries ; men rage and strive ;
They lift the voice for passion, power, and fame ;
They will and do, and through and by them, still
Unrecked of and unknown, He wills and does,
And slowly and most surely in this world
His kingdom groweth on !

Lift up your heads,
Ye brazen gates that long have shut Him out !
Be lifted up, O everlasting doors,
And let the King come in ! Most glorious time
When Jesus shall be King, and He alone !
When Mars shall die and Mammon hide her face ;
Oppression, Bribery, and bitter Wrong—
The false gods and usurpers !

THE UNSEEN KINGDOM.

        Lord, how long !
How long before Thy saints, the meek of earth,
Beneath the whole broad heavens shall reign with Thee ?
Our souls are faint with waiting, while the blood
Reaches the horses' bridles ! So we cry :
But Thou art calm on Thine eternal throne ;
Thy patience wearies not ; Thy word is sure ;
And though the vision tarry, it will come ;—
The kingdoms of this world shall all become
The kingdoms of our Lord and of His Christ !
Rejoice and break out into singing, Earth !
Forever and forever He shall reign !

AMONG THE RUSHES.

WHERE the lotus-leaves are floating,
    Where the quiet waters creep,
In a cradle wrought of rushes
    Lies a little babe asleep.

In the poor home of a bondman
    Prays the mother, sobbing wild:
"Save him, O thou great Jehovah!
    Save and keep my little child!

"Save him from the King of Egypt,
    Cruel as the crocodile!"
While she prays the morning reddens,
    Shining on the river Nile.

Downward through the sloping gardens
    Come the ladies of the court;
Watching through the large-leaved branches
    Miriam hears them laugh and sport.

Hears the princess' exclamation ;
   Sees the maidens turn their eyes
Where the precious little casket
   'Mong the river-rushes lies.

Now they bear it to their lady ;
   (Miriam holds her breath to hear) ;
Now she lifts the cover lightly ;
   Now the maidens gather near.

" He is fairer than a dovelet !
   Lovelier than the rising day ! "
" Mark his little pouting rose-lips,
   Mark his dimpled hands, I pray ! "

" He is sweeter than a lily !
   Graceful as a sleeping fawn ! "
" He 's a child-god of the morning,
   Rosy with the coming dawn ! "

" Lotus-flower upon the river ! "
   " Pearl within a slimy shell ! "
" Let me kiss his dainty fingers ! "
   " Let me kiss his lips as well ! "

So they woke the slumbering baby,
  But he shrank from each embrace,—
Turned from all the eager maidens,
  Grieving for his mother's face.

And the lips of budding roses
  Quivered with his baby fears;
And his eyes, divine in beauty,
  Filled and overflowed with tears.

" He must be a Hebrew infant,"
  Said the princess tenderly;
" Sweetest baby! nought shall harm you!
  You henceforth belong to me."

Near the group of wondering women,
  Trembling, hoping, Miriam drew,—
Humbly asked the royal lady:
  " Shall I call a nurse for you?"

" Go," the princess answered queenly;
  As on pinions Miriam went,
And the mother's look of question
  Answered with a glad content.

"Hasten to the palace garden,
   For the child is saved from death!"
Then they blessed the loving Father
   Who had heard the prayer of faith.

Yet they saw not how 't was written
   In the book of God's decree:
"He shall be a prince and leader;
   He shall set My people free!"

THE UNSEEN GUARD.

To his courtiers spake the monarch with trouble in
    his eye:
"Will ye tell us who among us is a traitor and a spy?
My stratagem is baffled, my ambush set at nought,—
Who tells the King of Israel the secret of my thought?"

Then answered back a courtier: "'T is none of us, O
    King;
But a prophet dwells in Israel who maketh known the
    thing;
Conferrings in thy council with chosen friends apart,
Thy words within thy chamber and thy thoughts within
    thy heart."

Then spake the king in anger: "Go, spy where he may
    be;
Take chariots and horsemen, and bring him back to me."
The servant of Elisha rose up at break of day,
And lo, about the city the host of Syria lay!

He sought in haste his master, his lips were white with
    fear :
"Alas, for we are taken ! the Syrians are here !
How shall we do, my master?" Elisha calmly smiled,
Like one who sees, untroubled, the terror of a child.

"Fear not," he answered kindly, "for they that be with us
Are more than our beseigers"; he lifted, speaking thus,
His aged hands to heaven : "Lord, open Thou his eyes!"
The prayer had instant answer, and starting with surprise,
The young man saw the mountain as 't were with fire
    alight,
And a vast and wondrous army flashed glory on his sight.

With white resplendent horses went the chariots and the
    cars,
And the gems upon the bridles had the splendor of the
    stars ;
Of the color of the lightning were the chariots every one,
And they that stood within them wore armor like the sun !
And the triumph of their music thrilled the listener like a
    shout,
For legion upon legion of the hosts of God were out !

"O blind and foolish Syrians! Return the way ye came!"
Bewildered and mistaken they think they see and know;
The prophet thus they follow as sheep to slaughter go;
He leads them to Samaria, to the army of their foe.
"My father, shall I smite them?" the king of Israel said.
"Nay, nay," Elisha answered, "but set before them bread,
And thus refreshed, the captives back to their master send."
So did the king of Israel,—and so the war had end.

Full oft we read the story as something passed away
All in the vanished ages,—unheeding that to-day,
Invisible and countless, with flashing swords of flame
The host of God encampeth 'round those that fear His name.

AMONG THE LIONS.

"PROPHET!" said the monarch,
  "The night went ill with me;
No slumber closed my eyelids,
  For I only thought of thee.
I loathed the dainty banquet;
  From the wine I turned away;
The singing girls I banished,
  And I longed to see the day.

"The gods of every country
  I petitioned every hour;
Then there came to mind thy saying,
  That thy God alone had power,—
Jehovah of the Hebrews!
  So I called upon His name
Till tardily and sullenly
  The gray of morning came.

" Then, sickening with the odor
   Of spice-lamps burning low,
I left the royal chamber
   Beneath the skies to go.
The moon was sinking slowly;
   The stars were dying out;
I sought the den of lions,
   Half maddened with the doubt.

"I called upon thee loudly
   Above the den of blood;
I held my breath and listened;
   I trembled as I stood.
'O Monarch! live forever!'
   I scarce believed for bliss!
Ne'er sounded salutation
   In kingly ear like this!

" Thine enemies have perished,
   And thou art safe at last;
I fain would hear thy story,
   How the night with thee was passed."

Then Daniel answered slowly,
   With a quiet, holy smile,
Like one who seeth further
   Than he telleth, all the while :

"All night among the lions
   I knelt upon the ground ;
Like sheep a shepherd foldeth
   They calmly lay around.
For I saw an angel 'mong them
   As I fell adown the height,
And the brightness of his raiment
   Filled the gloomy den with light.

"The fierce and bloody lions,
   At his voice, like music sweet,
Crouched low and fawned before him,
   And slept beside his feet.
Then I knew not, for a season,
   If my spirit had gone free,
Or, still among the lions,
   God's heaven had come to me.

" For a vision full of glory
    Took possession of my soul,
And I heard a strain of triumph,
    An anthem's solemn roll ;
The pæan of the planets
    At the feet of God I heard ;
And the voices of the ages
    That are waiting for His word :

" The far-off, future ages,
    When Shiloh having birth—
The Shiloh of the nations—
    He shall have His right on earth.
And the glorious Living Creatures
    Were passing in my sight,
That do their earth-work nightly,
    And come and go like light.

" Till I heard thee say : ' O Daniel,
    Who serv'st the living Lord,
Is He able to deliver
    According to thy word ? '

So the glorious vision vanished
　　And darkness o'er me swept,
And I heard the heavy breathing
　　Of the lions as they slept.

"Jehovah, King of nations,
　　This message sends to thee:
'My servant I deliver
　　Because he trusts in Me.
Among the gods thou soughtest,
　　I heard and saw alone;
I reign in earth and heaven,
　　And beside Me there is none.
When with sorrow or with danger
　　The sons of men I prove,
I hasten to deliver
　　The soul that trusts My love.'"

THE VISIT OF THE ANGELS.

THE little lambs slept by their mothers
   All under the silver sky,
And they dreamed of the lilies that grew in the grass,
   And the waters that glided by.

By the stars on God's great dial
   It was midnight, solemn and calm ;
The shepherds sat on the gray old rocks
   And chanted this ancient psalm :

" In every land, Jehovah !
   Thy name is excellent !
The babes and sucklings praise Thee,
   And the starry firmament !

" When I behold Thy heavens,
   The work Thy hands have wrought,
Lord ! what is man the sinful,
   For whom Thou takest thought ?

THE VISIT OF THE ANGELS.

" A step below the angels
   Who all Thy glory see,
Thou crownest him with honor
   On earth to reign for Thee.

" Thou givest him dominion
   O'er all Thy flocks and herds,
O'er all that swim Thy waters,
   O'er all Thy beasts and birds.

" O Lord! our Lord Jehovah!
   Let all the earth proclaim
How great Thy power and glory,
   How excellent Thy name!"

Then over the chanting shepherds
   There suddenly flashed a light,
As though the glow of a myriad moons
   Was filling the lonesome night;
For wearing a glory that dimmed the stars
   Came an angel down the height!

" Fear not," he said, " but rejoice instead!"
   (For the men were sore afraid,

And unto the Lord of life and death
　　Each one in his terror prayed.)

"Fear not," he said, " but rejoice instead !"
　　And his voice like a flute-note fell ;
" I bring you tidings of greatest joy,—
　　For you, and the world as well !

" The Lord of glory has come to men,"—
　　And his tone grew high and clear,—
" For the Babe is born in Bethlehem,
　　And the Christ who should appear ! "

Then all at once with the angel
　　Was a marvellous company;
The sky was full of a shining host
　　That was singing an anthem high.

" Glory to God in the highest ! "
　　Were the words they heard them say ;
" Good-will toward men, and peace on earth,
　　And glory to God alway ! "

And still, as they floated higher,
  Till they vanished far up in the blue,
The burden of words that the shepherds caught
  Was "glory to God!" anew.

So they passed away to heaven,
  And the calm stars shone on high;
And still the little lambs lay asleep,
  And the water glided by.

THE BLESSED MASTER.

HIS hands were hardened with carpenters' tools;
    His sandals were dusty with going afoot;
He was all unlearned in the subtle schools;
    He was meek and lowly and destitute.

The fox in the hillside burrowed her home;
    The bird in the branches builded her bed;
The King of the earth to His kingdom come
    Owned never a roof to shelter His head.

But oh, the grace of His loving face!
    The touch of His tender hand!
What joy to stay by His side alway,
    As He went through all the land!

To hear His talk in the daily walk
    By the vineyard or the wheat,
To know He has blest the couch of our rest
    And the poorest food we eat!

ON THE WATER.

THE Master has sent His disciples away;
    He tarries alone in the mountain to pray:
They spread out their sail to the fresh coming wind,
But wistfully turn to the dark shore behind.

The firs and the cedars are black by the lake,
But silver in moonlight the little waves break,
The stars of the midnight already look out:
Still linger the sailors the dim strand about.

They wonder, they question: " Now why should this be?
And how shall the Master pass over the sea?"
They push out from land, but they pause on their way;
He comes not:—no longer they dare disobey.

But sad and reluctant, while plying the oar,
They are looking behind for some token from shore.
And now on the lake they are scarcely midway,
And morn in the east breaketh sullen and gray.

But fast o'er the sky scuds the wild tempest-cloud,
Then down comes the hurricane howling aloud!
The mad winds are all from their leashes let slip,
And Jesus the Master is not in the ship!

They take in the sail, and they say in their fear,
"The prince of the power of the air must be near!"
Now toiling in rowing they cry out in fright,
"A spirit is walking the waters to-night!"

There's a hush on the gale, and they hear a reply,
'T is the voice of the Master: "Fear not, it is I!"
The black hungry billows dash on to destroy,
But the hearts of the sailors are bounding with joy.

Like lilies in moonlight His white garments shine,
And the light of His face is a glory divine;
The little waves leap up, the dear Lord to greet,
And the white foam is kissing the dust from His feet!

Then Peter said boldly: "Lord, if it be Thou,
Command that I come on the waves to Thee now."
The Master says, "Come"; and his fisherman's coat
Throwing hastily round him, he steps from the boat.

And looking to Jesus he walks on the sea,
But the wind-tempest, laughing in wild jubilee,
Whirls up the great waves, and he cries out afraid :
" Lord, save me ! the waters go over my head ! "

And instantly Jesus His hand stretches out ;
He saves him ; He asks him : " Oh, why didst thou doubt ?
Oh why should thy faith be so weak as to think
I would call thee to ' Come ' and then leave thee to sink ? "

They enter the ship, and the trumpet-like shout
Of the gale, to the breath of a whisper dies out ;
The glad men fall down at the feet of the Lord,
And worship their Master—Messiah, the Word !

A SONG FOR SORROWFUL WOMEN.

 THOU who for gloom of the future
   Art pressed with the boding care,
And sick for the coming sorrow
   Dost utter the Master's prayer;

Come walk in the ancient Garden
   In the early morning dim;
The few large stars of the twilight
   Are singing their ceaseless hymn:

The small birds swing on the branches
   In the fresh day's new delight,
And the air is spiced with sweetness
   Where the flowers have dreamed all night.

But where the heart of the Garden
   Is heavy with evergreen fir,
With cypress rising behind it,
   There standeth a sepulchre.

And sorrowful women question,
　　As they enter the flowery way :
" Oh, who from the tomb of the Master
　　Shall roll us the stone ? " they say.

" And why should the joy of creation
　　Still rise with the incense-breath,
When the Lord of life and glory
　　Is sleeping the sleep of death ! "

O weeping and loving women !
　　Come see where the Master lay !
From the sepulchre *forever*
　　Has the stone been rolled away !

And He now walks in the Garden
　　Who hung on the cross above !
And the tender hands that were wounded
　　Are full of the gifts of love !

THE PRAYER-MEETING FOR PETER.

AT Mary's house the little church had met by night to pray,
For James was slain, and Peter still in chains and prison lay.
"And must Thy chosen band, dear Lord, be wasted thus away?
Dost care not if we perish, Lord? We cry for help to Thee!
For now, alas! our little bark is tossing out at sea,
And Peter sinks, unless Thy hand be stretched out instantly."

The pleader rises from his knees; another takes the word:
"We come to Thee in deep distress! Remember Peter, Lord!"
They start; upon the outer gate a sudden knock is heard!
The damsel Rhoda goes without, but comes with step elate;

"Now who," she cries, "but Peter's self before the house
    doth wait!"
For wild with joy, the child she was, she opened not the
    gate.

"Now, maiden, thou art surely mad!" a good old broth-
    er saith;—
'T was he who thought he prayed, just now, the holy
    prayer of faith,
Reaching the unseen hand that holds the keys of life and
    death.
But stronger still the girl affirmed, "It is as I have
    said";
Then each upon the other looked, and sadly shook the
    head;
"His angel, then, has come to us, and Peter now is
    dead!"

Again, and still again the knock, and some go out to
    see;
And, coming back,—'t is Peter's self doth bear them com-
    pany!

He beckoning them to hold their peace declared the
    mystery.
For, rising up, they all stood forth to take him by the
    hand,
And all began to speak at once what none might understand,
With eager question, kind salute, a joyful little band.

PETER'S STORY.

"I was chained between two soldiers,
    And the keepers kept the door;
But how vain are bolts and fetters
    When has come the Lord's good hour!
What is e'en the Roman legion
    To the angel of His power!

"I had thought: 'Another morning
    I shall know death's mystery,
And in glorious heavenly mansion
    I again my Lord shall see!
For on earth the blessed Master
    Hath no longer need of me.'

THE PRAYER-MEETING FOR PETER.

"As I slept, between the soldiers,
   Child-like slumber, soft and sweet,
Suddenly a heavenly being
   Touched and set me on my feet,
Softly saying, 'Rise up quickly.'
   Down my fetters noiseless came,
Like to ropes that Samson tested,
   Like to flax dissolved by flame.

"Then I saw the wondrous being
   Lighting all the heavy gloom,
For the stirring of his raiment
   Flashed a glory through the room;
Still I thought that I was dreaming
   In my dreary prison-tomb.

"'Gird thyself, bind on thy sandals,
   Take thy garment, follow me';
Thus he spake, and still the soldiers
   Lay and slumbered heavily:
Passing on, my leader led me
   Through the first and second ward;

Then the heavy gate of iron
    Opened of its own accord.
Still I said : 'I yet am dreaming ;
    'T is a vision from my Lord !'

" Passing all the guards and keepers,
    Following close my leader bright,
In a well-known street I found me ;
    Then he vanished from my sight.
Lo ! about me lay the city ;
    O'er my head the starry night.

"' So,' I said, 'I am not dreaming !'
    And for awe I held my breath !
' God has sent His holy angel
    And delivered me from death !
Still He needs me for His harvest ;
    Still He doth my life refuse
To the cruel hate of Herod
    And the malice of the Jews.' "

I WISHED MYSELF AMONG THEM.

 WISHED myself among them ! In the dashing and the roar
I struggled till I fainted for the green and quiet shore :
The waves forever tossing, and the wind a maddened shout ;
The haunting voice within me, and the phantom eyes without !

O God, to be among them ! where the sea has passed away,
The sorrow and the crying, the wrestling and affray !
Where the glory hath no shadow, and the music brings no pain,
And the lost ones of our bosom return to us again !

Where the radiant eyes around us are brimming all with love !

And the beating heart keeps measure to the breathing of
    the Dove !
Where every tongue is singing, and our Saviour is the
    song !
O God, to be among them ! the pilgrim way is long !

THE LORD'S DAY.

FALLING half asleep, some spirit
    Seems to take me by the hand,
Suddenly, without transition,
    To a radiant summer-land;
Where the light is like a glory,
    Where the mountains are sublime,
And the feet of young immortals
    Rather seem to fly than climb.

Trees are there, like palms in stature;
    Birds of shape and plumage rare,
Streaked and hued like gorgeous lilies,
    Float along the ambient air.
Then a voice, a stir, awakes me;
    I am on a couch of pain;
And this weak and weary body
    Holds me like an iron chain.

Hark ! the robins in the linden !
   Hark ! the swallows in the sun !
Singing for the joy of living !
   Bliss of being just begun !
Hark ! the Lord's day chimes are playing !
   List the sound of joyful feet
Passing onward to the temples
   Where the Lord's belovèd meet !

Lo ! another Lord's day cometh !
   Soon for me it may be here !
All my heart leaps up in gladness
   When I think it draweth near !
Every fetter fallen from me
   In His countenance divine,
I shall see Him in His beauty,
   Mary's risen Lord and mine !

OUT OF THE NIGHT.

WHAT though we are late in the cold, starless night,
   Still nearer we draw to our own Father's door;
And out from the tempest and into the light
   We surely shall come when our journey is o'er.

The burdens that crush us well-nigh to the dust,
   The anguish that tortures, the terrors and fears,
Are known to the Heart in whose love we may trust,
   That watcheth our stumbling, that counteth our tears.

The way groweth lonely, the sky is more drear,
   The helpers who loved us have passed through the tomb;
But He who is mightiest still is most near;
   Let us reach forth our hand and meet His in the gloom.

The false fires are dancing to dazzle our sight;
   There is danger around, there is darkness before.
But look! through the casement doth shine out the light,
   As nearer we draw to our own Father's door!

TWENTY-FOUR AND SIXTY.

AT TWENTY-FOUR.

"ADIEU is a mournful word," you say;
    Your sigh has a heart-break sound;
But friends who go will return again,
    The world is a merry-go-round.

I am turning the leaves of my book of life,
    I have read just twenty-four,
And the story is far more wonderful
    Than it was at half a score.

And finer and richer still it grows,
    And grief is never the text,
And my pulses thrill, and I hold my breath,
    As I wonder what is next.

The opal stone is the gem for me,
    And I take the world as it goes;
The snow-drop dies, and the daffodil;
    We are yet to have the rose!

AT SIXTY.

How long ago the roses died !
    The lilies long have left the lakes ;
The royal Summer's wealth and pride
    Passed like a dream when one awakes.

The trees have lost the flush of fruit ;
    The night is crowding on the day ;
The maples miss the robin's flute ;
    Only the tiresome sparrows stay.

But star-flowers in the graveyard grow,
    And all the Autumn air is gold ;
And look ! the night-skies are aglow
    With constellations grand and old !

The friends who went returned no more ;
    But why should I be therefore vexed ?
I watch the opening of the door,
    And wait in trust what may be next.

www.ingramcontent.com/pod-product-compliance
Lightning Source LLC
Chambersburg PA
CBHW030312170426
43202CB00009B/971